Understanding Commodity Futures Markets

Roggie Clark

Continue Learning At Our Website: Roggieclarkbooks.com

Continue exploring educational resources, tools, books, workbooks, and learning materials designed to help readers continue building knowledge and practical skills. Visit: www.roggieclarkbooks.com

Inside you'll find:

- Educational worksheets
- Beginner-friendly guides
- Printable activities
- Companion materials for books and courses

A growing library of educational content for readers, collectors, learners, parents, teachers, and lifelong students.

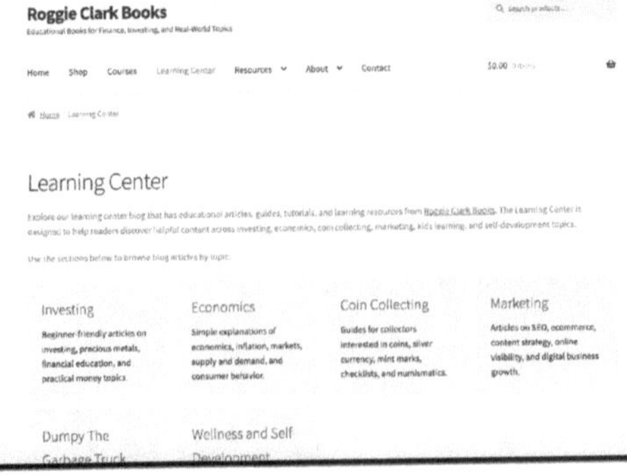

The Strategic Guide to U.S. Mint Gold and Silver Coin Investing

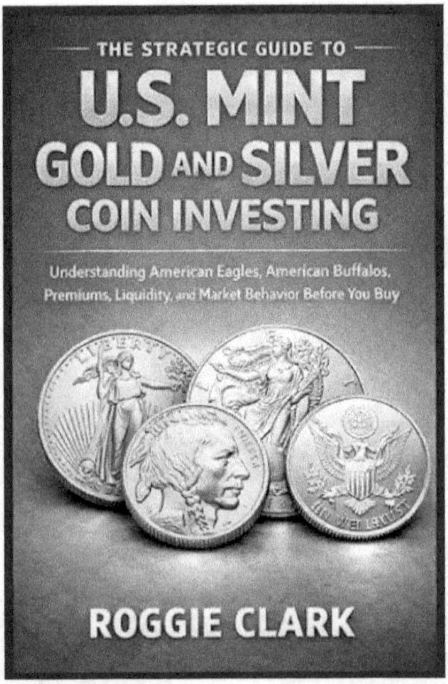

Rather than offering a general introduction to precious metals, this guide examines how American Gold Eagles, American Gold Buffalos, and Silver American Eagles behave in real investor markets.

https://www.amazon.com/Strategic-Guide-U-S-Silver-Investing/dp/B0GQKJF9K6

Copyright

Title: Understanding Commodity Futures Markets
Author: Roggie Clark

Cover Design: Roggie Clark
Editing: Renee' Clark

Printed in the United States of America

Disclaimer

The views and opinions expressed in this publication are those of the author and do not necessarily reflect the official policies, positions, opinions, or viewpoints of any individual, company, organization, institution, agency, or entity referenced or mentioned within this work.

The author is not necessarily affiliated with, endorsed by, sponsored by, or compensated by any individuals, companies, organizations, brands, institutions, products, or services referenced within this publication unless specifically stated otherwise. Any examples, sample situations, stories, illustrations, or scenarios presented may be fictionalized or simplified for educational purposes. Any resemblance to actual persons, living or dead, businesses, or events is purely coincidental unless otherwise stated.

The information, ideas, strategies, concepts, techniques, opinions, suggestions, and educational materials contained in this publication are provided on an "as is" basis without warranties of any kind, either express or implied. While every effort has been made to provide accurate and current information, neither the author nor the publisher makes any representations or warranties regarding the completeness, accuracy, reliability, suitability, or applicability of the information presented.

This publication is intended solely for educational and informational purposes and should not be interpreted as professional advice of any kind, including but not limited to financial, investment, legal, tax, business, medical, mental health, educational, psychological, or other professional guidance. Readers should conduct their own independent research and consult appropriately qualified professionals before making decisions that may affect their finances, health, business, education, legal matters, personal circumstances, or other important areas of life.

Results, outcomes, and experiences may vary significantly among individuals. Neither the author nor the publisher guarantees any specific outcomes, results, earnings, performance improvements, personal achievements, or benefits resulting from the use of information contained in this publication.

By reading, accessing, or using this publication, you acknowledge and agree that the author and publisher shall not be held liable for any direct, indirect, incidental, consequential, financial, personal, emotional, or other damages, losses, or claims arising from the use, misuse, interpretation, or application of information contained within this publication. You assume full responsibility for any actions, decisions, and outcomes resulting from the use of this material.

Image Credits and Public Domain Notice

All images, illustrations, graphics, photographs, visual references, and related materials included in this publication are believed to be in the public domain, used under applicable licenses or permissions, created by the author or publisher, or obtained from sources that clearly identify them as available for lawful use.

The author and publisher have made a good faith effort to use only visual materials that are lawfully available for use and distribution. Where applicable, images and visual materials may have been resized, cropped, edited, enhanced, stylized, modified, reformatted, or arranged for educational, informational, design, formatting, or presentation purposes.

This publication is intended for educational, informational, and illustrative purposes only. The inclusion of any image, artwork, photograph, visual reference, symbol, historical material, design, or graphic element is not intended to claim ownership over public domain materials or any third-party intellectual property rights that remain with their respective owners.

If you believe any image or visual material included in this publication has been used in error, please contact the author or publisher so the matter may be reviewed and corrected in future editions or releases if necessary.

Any factual information, specifications, historical references, values, descriptions, statistics, or related content accompanying visual materials are provided for general informational purposes only and may change over time. Readers should conduct their own independent research and consult appropriate sources or qualified professionals when making decisions based on information presented in this publication.

This publication is independently produced and is not affiliated with, endorsed by, sponsored by, or associated with any company, organization, government agency, institution, trademark holder, or third party unless specifically stated otherwise.

Table of Contents

- Introduction: Understanding the Role of Commodity Futures
- Chapter 1: How Commodity Futures Contracts Work
- Chapter 2: Pricing and Price Discovery
- Chapter 3: Hedging and Speculation
- Chapter 4: Margin, Leverage, and Risk
- Chapter 5: Energy, Metals, and Agricultural Futures
- Chapter 6: What Moves Commodity Futures Markets
- Last Thoughts: Understanding Futures Before Participating

Introduction: Understanding the Role of Commodity Futures

Commodity futures markets connect the financial world with the physical goods used throughout the global economy. Oil producers, farmers, mining companies, manufacturers, food processors, financial institutions, and traders can all participate in these markets for very different reasons. Some want protection from changing prices. Others accept price risk in pursuit of potential profits. Understanding how these participants interact provides the foundation for understanding why commodity futures exist and why their prices matter far beyond the trading screen.

Why Commodity Futures Markets Exist

Commodity prices can change significantly between the time something is produced and the time it is eventually sold or purchased.

Consider a farmer planting corn.

The farmer may spend months paying for seeds, fertilizer, equipment, fuel, labor, and other expenses before the crop is ready for sale. During that period, the market price of corn could rise or fall.

A significant decline could reduce the farmer's expected revenue.

A food manufacturer faces the opposite problem. If the company expects to purchase large quantities of corn several months from now, a sharp increase in prices could raise its production costs.

Both businesses face **price risk**, but from different directions.

Commodity futures markets provide a way to manage some of that uncertainty.

A **futures contract** is a standardized agreement involving the purchase or sale of a particular commodity at a specified price for a future period. These contracts trade on organized futures exchanges and follow defined rules covering matters such as contract size, quality specifications, expiration, and settlement.

Futures allow market participants to establish prices today for transactions connected to future periods.

This does not eliminate every business risk. Production can still change. Demand can fall. Transportation problems can occur. Weather can damage crops. Companies can experience financial difficulties.

What futures can do is help separate some of the uncertainty surrounding commodity prices from the other risks of running a business.

That function is one of the primary reasons futures markets developed.

But modern futures markets serve another purpose as well.

They allow thousands of participants to continuously express their expectations about future commodity prices. As those expectations change, futures prices adjust.

The result is a market that performs both a **risk-transfer function** and an information function.

Connecting Financial Markets to Physical Commodities

Commodity futures are financial contracts, but the markets underlying them are very physical.

Crude oil must be extracted, transported, refined, and stored.

Copper must be mined, processed, transported, and eventually used by manufacturers.

Corn and wheat must be planted, harvested, stored, and shipped.

These physical realities influence futures prices.

A drought affecting a major agricultural region can change expectations for crop supplies. Political instability in an important oil-producing region can affect expectations about energy availability. Strong construction or manufacturing activity can increase expectations for industrial metal demand.

Inventories matter as well.

When large supplies of a commodity are available in storage, buyers may have more flexibility. When inventories become unusually low, concerns about shortages can make markets more sensitive to disruptions.

This relationship between physical supply and financial pricing makes commodity futures different from many other financial markets.

A share of stock represents ownership in a company. A bond represents a lending relationship. A commodity futures contract is tied to expectations surrounding a physical market.

That does not mean every futures trader intends to receive barrels of oil or truckloads of grain.

Many futures positions are closed before expiration. Some contracts are also settled financially rather than through physical delivery.

However, the possibility of settlement and the connection to the underlying commodity help keep futures prices connected to physical market conditions.

This is why understanding commodity futures requires more than watching prices move on a chart.

Supply, demand, inventories, transportation, storage, production costs, weather, geopolitics, currencies, and economic activity can all become relevant.

Futures markets take information about these conditions and translate changing expectations into prices.

This process contributes to **price discovery**, where buyers and sellers collectively establish market prices through their transactions.

Those prices can become important reference points throughout the physical economy.

Hedgers, Speculators, and Other Market Participants

Not everyone participating in commodity futures markets has the same objective.

One of the most important groups consists of **hedgers**.

Hedgers generally participate because they already face commodity price exposure through their businesses.

A producer may be concerned about falling prices.

A commercial buyer may be concerned about rising prices.

Using futures can allow these participants to offset some of their exposure.

For example, a producer expecting to sell a commodity in the future may establish a futures position intended to provide some protection if prices decline. A business expecting to purchase a commodity may use futures differently to reduce its exposure to rising prices.

The objective is not necessarily to earn a trading profit.

The objective is to make future costs or revenues more predictable.

Another major group consists of **speculators**.

Speculators generally accept price risk because they believe they can profit from changes in futures prices. They may analyze supply and demand, economic conditions, price trends, weather, geopolitical developments, or other information when deciding whether to participate.

Although speculation is sometimes described negatively, speculators perform an important market function.

A hedger trying to reduce risk needs another participant willing to accept that risk.

Speculators can provide that willingness.

They can also contribute to **market liquidity**, making it easier for participants to buy and sell contracts without causing unusually large price changes.

Commodity futures markets can include many other participants as well, including financial institutions, investment funds, trading firms, commodity merchants, and professional market makers.

Their motivations can vary considerably.

Some may hedge. Some may speculate. Some may attempt to profit from price differences between related markets. Others may use commodities as part of broader investment strategies.

Understanding these different motivations is important because futures markets are not simply places where traders make predictions about prices.

They are marketplaces where participants with different economic needs transfer risk between one another.

That transfer is central to the entire futures system.

Last Thoughts

Commodity futures markets exist because commodity prices are uncertain and that uncertainty creates real economic consequences for producers, businesses, and market participants. Futures provide a structured marketplace where price risk can be transferred, future expectations can be reflected in prices, and participants with very different objectives can trade with one another. Understanding the distinction between **physical commodities, futures contracts, hedgers, and speculators** provides the foundation for everything that follows. The next chapter will examine the futures contract itself, including how contracts are standardized, how expiration and settlement work, and how futures prices relate to prices in the physical market.

Chapter 1: How Commodity Futures Contracts Work

Commodity futures markets depend on contracts that establish clear rules for buyers and sellers. Instead of negotiating every detail of every transaction individually, futures exchanges create standardized contracts that define the commodity, quantity, expiration period, and other important terms. This structure makes it possible for large numbers of participants to trade commodity price exposure efficiently without requiring most traders to handle the physical commodity itself.

Futures Contracts, Exchanges, and Standardization

A futures contract represents an agreement tied to the future purchase or sale of an underlying commodity.

Unlike a privately negotiated agreement between two businesses, exchange-traded futures follow standardized specifications.

Standardization means that the exchange establishes many of the important characteristics of the contract before trading begins.

These specifications can include:

- The quantity represented by one contract
- The acceptable quality or grade of the commodity
- The contract months available for trading
- The procedures for settlement
- The approved delivery locations when physical delivery applies
- The minimum amount by which the quoted price can change

Consider an agricultural commodity.

Without standardization, one trader might be offering one quantity and quality while another trader expects something entirely different. Establishing uniform contract specifications allows market participants to focus primarily on the price.

Futures exchanges provide the organized marketplaces where these contracts trade.

The exchange does not simply provide a place for buyers and sellers to meet. Futures markets also rely on clearing systems that help manage obligations between participants.

A **clearinghouse** effectively stands between buyers and sellers after trades are executed. Rather than each participant depending entirely on the financial reliability of an unknown person on the opposite side of a transaction, the clearing process establishes rules for maintaining positions and meeting financial obligations.

This system is one reason margin requirements are important in futures markets, a subject we will examine more closely later in the book.

Standardization also makes contracts easier to trade.

A participant who buys a standardized futures contract does not usually need to locate the original seller later to exit the position. The trader can generally establish an offsetting position in the same contract.

This ability helps create active markets where contracts can change hands many times before expiration.

Contract Size, Expiration, and Settlement

Every futures contract represents a specific quantity of its underlying commodity.

This is known as the **contract size**.

The appropriate unit depends on the market. Energy contracts may be based on quantities of fuel, agricultural contracts may represent quantities of grain, and metals contracts may represent specified weights.

Contract size is important because it determines the amount of commodity exposure represented by a single position.

If a futures price changes, the financial effect on the trader depends on both the size of the price movement and the quantity represented by the contract.

Futures contracts also have expiration periods.

Rather than trading one permanent contract for a commodity, markets generally offer contracts associated with different future months.

A business may be concerned about commodity prices several months from now, while another participant may be focused on a much nearer period. Different contract months allow these participants to trade exposure connected to different points in time.

As expiration approaches, traders must decide what to do with their positions.

Many participants close their futures positions before reaching the settlement process.

Others may move their exposure into a later contract, a process commonly called **rolling a position**.

For contracts that permit physical delivery, participants remaining in qualifying positions through the appropriate period may become involved in the delivery process.

Physical settlement does not usually mean that a casual trader suddenly receives a commodity without warning. Exchanges and brokerage firms maintain detailed rules surrounding delivery, and traders need to understand those rules before holding contracts close to expiration.

Other futures contracts use **cash settlement**.

Instead of transferring the physical commodity, the financial difference is settled according to the rules of the contract.

Whether settlement is physical or financial, expiration matters because futures contracts are not designed to exist indefinitely.

This distinguishes them from assets such as common stocks, which generally do not have expiration dates.

Spot Prices Versus Futures Prices

Understanding futures markets also requires understanding the difference between prices for commodities today and prices associated with future periods.

The **spot price** generally refers to the current price associated with the physical commodity for near-term transactions.

A futures price represents the market price of a futures contract connected to a specified future period.

These prices do not have to be identical.

Suppose a commodity is available today, but a buyer wants exposure to its price several months from now. Holding the physical commodity until then could involve storage, insurance, financing, transportation, and other costs.

Market expectations can also change the relationship.

Participants may expect future supplies to increase or decrease. They may anticipate stronger demand, weaker economic activity, favorable harvests, production disruptions, or changes in inventories.

As a result, futures contracts for different expiration months can trade at different prices.

Together, these prices form a **futures curve**.

The shape of that curve can provide information about current market conditions and expectations across different time periods.

However, futures prices should not be interpreted as guaranteed predictions of what the spot price will eventually become.

Unexpected events can change commodity markets quickly.

Weather can alter agricultural production. Political events can affect energy supplies. Economic conditions can change industrial demand. New production can enter the market, or transportation problems can prevent existing supplies from reaching buyers.

As new information arrives, futures prices adjust.

One important relationship becomes increasingly relevant as a contract approaches expiration.

The futures price and the corresponding physical market price generally become more closely connected as the settlement period approaches. Without this relationship, significant pricing differences could create opportunities for market participants to exploit inconsistencies between the two markets.

This connection helps keep futures markets tied to the physical commodities they represent.

Later, we will examine situations where futures prices for later months are above or below nearer prices. These structures, known as contango and backwardation, can reveal important information about inventories, storage, supply, demand, and market conditions.

Last Thoughts

Commodity futures contracts work because exchanges establish standardized rules that allow many different participants to trade the same instruments. Contract specifications define what is being traded, expiration establishes when the agreement reaches its endpoint, and settlement determines how remaining obligations are resolved. At the same time, the relationship between spot and futures prices keeps these financial contracts connected to physical commodity markets. Understanding this structure makes it possible to move to the next question: **how futures prices are actually formed and what those prices can tell us about supply, demand, inventories, storage, and expectations for the future.**

Chapter 2: Pricing and Price Discovery

Commodity futures prices are constantly adjusting as buyers and sellers respond to new information. A change in weather, inventories, production, transportation, economic activity, or geopolitical conditions can alter expectations about future supply and demand. Futures markets bring these expectations together, creating prices for different delivery periods and providing information that producers, businesses, traders, and other market participants can use when making decisions.

How Futures Markets Discover Prices

Price discovery occurs through the interaction of buyers and sellers.

Some participants believe a commodity is undervalued and are willing to buy futures contracts. Others believe prices may decline and are willing to sell. Commercial businesses may enter the market because they need to manage an existing price exposure rather than because they are attempting to predict the next market move.

All of these orders contribute to the market price.

This continuous interaction creates a **market-clearing price**, where available buying and selling interest can meet.

The process is constantly changing.

Suppose expectations develop that a major oil-producing region could experience a supply disruption. Traders may begin bidding energy futures higher before any actual shortage occurs because the market is incorporating the possibility of reduced future supply.

Agricultural markets can behave similarly.

If weather forecasts suggest conditions that could damage a major crop, futures prices may begin changing months before the final harvest is known.

The reverse can also happen.

Expectations of abundant production, slowing economic activity, or weaker demand can pressure futures prices before those conditions are fully reflected in physical markets.

This forward-looking characteristic makes commodity futures important sources of information.

However, a futures price should not be interpreted as a perfect forecast.

It represents the price at which participants are currently willing to trade based on the information, expectations, risks, and incentives available at that moment.

New information can quickly change those expectations.

Price discovery is therefore an ongoing process rather than a final prediction about what a commodity will eventually be worth.

Supply, Demand, Inventories, and Storage

Physical supply and demand remain fundamental forces in commodity markets.

Commodity supply can be influenced by production capacity, weather, mining output, crop yields, drilling activity, transportation networks, government policies, and many other factors.

Demand can depend on economic growth, consumer behavior, manufacturing activity, energy consumption, technology, seasonal patterns, and substitution between different commodities.

The relationship between the two helps determine whether a market has abundant supplies or faces potential shortages.

Inventories provide another important piece of information.

Stored commodities can act as a buffer between current production and current consumption.

If production temporarily exceeds demand, inventories may rise.

If consumption exceeds new supply, inventories can decline as stored commodities are used to meet demand.

This makes **inventory levels** particularly important in many futures markets.

High inventories can provide buyers with protection against temporary supply disruptions. Extremely low inventories can make markets more sensitive because there may be less material available to absorb unexpected shortages.

Storage is not free.

Physical commodities may require warehouses, tanks, security, insurance, transportation, financing, and maintenance. Some commodities are relatively easy to store for extended periods, while others can deteriorate or require specialized facilities.

These **carrying costs** can influence the relationship between current and future prices.

Interest rates can matter as well because money tied up in stored inventory has a financing cost.

The ability to store a commodity also differs dramatically between markets.

Metals can often be stored for long periods. Oil can be stored, but doing so requires tanks, terminals, ships, or other infrastructure. Agricultural products have quality and storage considerations.

Electricity is an even more unusual commodity because large-scale storage has historically been much more difficult than storing barrels of oil or tons of metal, although battery technology is changing parts of that market.

These physical differences help explain why commodity futures cannot all be analyzed in exactly the same way.

Understanding Contango and Backwardation

Looking at prices across different contract months can reveal important information about a commodity market.

One common market structure is **contango**.

Contango occurs when futures contracts for later periods trade at higher prices than nearer contracts.

For example, a commodity available for near-term delivery might trade below a contract representing delivery several months later.

Storage and financing costs can contribute to this structure.

If someone purchases a physical commodity today and stores it for future use, that person may incur storage, insurance, financing, and other expenses. Those costs can help support higher prices for later delivery.

Contango can also appear when near-term supplies are plentiful relative to immediate demand.

The opposite structure is **backwardation**.

Backwardation occurs when nearer futures contracts trade at higher prices than contracts for later periods.

This can happen when buyers place particularly high value on having access to a commodity now.

Low inventories, strong immediate demand, transportation problems, production disruptions, or concerns about shortages can contribute to this situation.

Consider a market experiencing an unexpected supply interruption.

Businesses that need the physical commodity immediately may be willing to pay more for near-term availability. At the same time, traders may expect the disruption to be resolved several months later.

Nearer contracts could therefore trade above later contracts.

Neither contango nor backwardation automatically tells traders what prices will do next.

A market in contango can remain in contango, become more pronounced, flatten, or move into backwardation. The same is true in reverse.

Instead, these structures provide information about the relationship between prices at different points in time.

They can also affect participants who maintain futures exposure for extended periods.

Because individual futures contracts expire, a participant who wants continuous exposure may need to close an approaching contract and establish a position in a later one. The price relationship between those contracts can affect the economics of maintaining that exposure.

Understanding the futures curve is therefore important not only for interpreting commodity conditions but also for understanding how longer-term futures positions behave.

Last Thoughts

Commodity futures prices reflect a continuous process in which participants respond to changing expectations about physical markets. Supply and demand provide the foundation, while inventories, storage costs, financing, transportation, and expectations about future conditions help shape prices across different contract months. Contango and backwardation provide additional insight into how the market values commodities across time. These pricing relationships become even more meaningful once we understand **why different participants enter futures markets in the first place**. The next chapter will examine how hedgers use futures to manage existing price exposure, why speculators willingly accept that risk, and how both groups contribute to functioning commodity markets.

Chapter 3: Hedging and Speculation

Commodity futures markets bring together participants with very different goals. A farmer may want protection from falling crop prices, while a manufacturer may be concerned about rising raw material costs. At the same time, traders may willingly accept exposure to those price movements because they believe they can profit from them. This interaction between hedging and speculation is one of the fundamental mechanisms that allows futures markets to transfer price risk.

Why Producers and Businesses Hedge

Businesses involved with physical commodities regularly face prices they cannot completely control.

A farmer may know approximately how much wheat will be harvested but not what the market price will be when the crop is sold.

A mining company may expect to produce copper over the coming months while worrying that copper prices could decline before the metal reaches buyers.

A manufacturer can face the opposite problem.

If a company requires large quantities of a commodity as an input, rising prices could increase production costs and reduce profit margins.

Businesses can use futures to reduce some of this uncertainty through **hedging**.

Consider a producer concerned about falling prices.

The producer could sell futures contracts associated with the period when the commodity is expected to be sold. If the commodity price later declines, the physical product may generate less revenue, but gains on the futures position could offset some of that decline.

A commercial buyer can approach the problem from the opposite direction.

If a business is concerned that a necessary commodity will become more expensive, it may buy futures contracts. If prices subsequently rise, gains on the futures position could help offset the higher cost of purchasing the physical commodity.

The purpose of these positions is not necessarily to outperform the market.

Hedging is primarily about **reducing price uncertainty**.

There are limitations.

A futures contract may not perfectly match the exact commodity, quality, location, quantity, or timing involved in a company's physical transaction. This difference can create **basis risk**, meaning the physical price and futures price may not move in exactly the same way.

Companies must therefore determine how much exposure they want to hedge and which contracts most closely match their actual risks.

Some businesses hedge only a portion of expected production or purchases. Others may hedge different amounts at different times.

A hedge can also create an opportunity cost. If a producer protects against falling prices and prices instead rise sharply, the futures position can offset some of the benefit from higher physical prices.

That does not necessarily mean the hedge failed.

If the original objective was to create greater predictability, the hedge may have accomplished exactly what the business intended.

The Role of Speculators

A hedger generally enters the futures market because of an existing economic exposure. A speculator enters primarily because of an expectation about prices.

A **speculative position** attempts to benefit from future price movements.

A trader expecting crude oil prices to rise might establish a long futures position. A trader expecting prices to decline might establish a short position.

Speculators can base these decisions on many forms of analysis.

Some study production and consumption. Others follow inventories, weather forecasts, economic data, currencies, geopolitical developments, or market trends.

Their expectations can be wrong.

If prices move in the opposite direction, speculators can lose money, and the leverage available in futures markets can make those losses substantial.

Despite this risk, speculation performs an important economic function.

Futures markets need participants willing to take the opposite side of transactions.

Imagine that many agricultural producers want protection from falling prices. Those producers may want to sell futures.

For those transactions to occur, buyers must exist on the other side.

Some buyers could be commercial users hedging against rising prices. Others could be speculators who believe prices will increase.

Speculators therefore help provide **liquidity** to futures markets.

Greater liquidity can make it easier for participants to enter and exit positions while reducing the effect an individual transaction has on market prices.

Speculators also participate in price discovery.

When traders analyze available information and act on their expectations, their buying and selling contributes to the prices observed throughout the market.

This does not mean speculation always improves markets or that speculative activity cannot become excessive.

Futures prices can experience rapid movements, periods of extreme optimism or pessimism, and changes in positioning that temporarily influence market behavior.

The important point is that speculation is not separate from the functioning of futures markets. It is one of the mechanisms through which risk is accepted, liquidity is provided, and differing expectations are expressed.

How Hedging and Speculation Interact

Hedgers and speculators may appear to have opposing goals, but their activities can complement one another.

Hedgers often want to transfer unwanted price risk.

Speculators are willing to accept price risk in pursuit of potential returns.

This creates a **risk-transfer relationship**.

Consider an oil producer worried about falling prices.

The producer may sell futures to establish greater certainty around future revenue. A trader who believes oil prices will rise might willingly take the opposite position.

Both participants enter the same market, but they do so for different reasons.

If oil prices decline, the producer's futures position can provide some protection while the speculative buyer may experience a loss.

If prices rise, the trader may profit while the producer's futures position may lose value. However, the producer may simultaneously receive a higher price for the physical oil.

Looking only at the futures position would therefore provide an incomplete picture of the hedger's outcome.

This distinction is essential.

A speculative position is usually evaluated largely according to whether it generates a trading gain or loss.

A hedge should generally be evaluated alongside the physical exposure it was intended to protect.

Other participants can create even more complex interactions.

Trading firms may attempt to profit from differences between related commodities or contract months. Financial institutions may manage exposure across several markets. Commodity merchants may simultaneously participate in physical trading, transportation, storage, and futures markets.

The result is an ecosystem in which commercial needs and financial activity continuously interact.

That interaction is one reason commodity futures markets can process enormous amounts of information.

Producers bring knowledge about production conditions. Commercial buyers bring information about demand. Traders respond to economic data and expectations. Storage operators react to inventory conditions. Other participants evaluate relationships between markets and contract months.

Their decisions collectively contribute to market prices.

However, accepting price risk through futures comes with an important feature that separates these contracts from simply purchasing many traditional investments: relatively small amounts of capital can control much larger amounts of commodity exposure.

That is where margin and leverage become especially important.

Last Thoughts

Hedging and speculation represent two different reasons for participating in commodity futures markets. Producers and businesses can use futures to reduce uncertainty surrounding prices they already face, while speculators willingly accept price exposure in pursuit of potential returns. Together, these participants contribute to liquidity, price discovery, and the transfer of risk throughout commodity markets. Neither activity removes risk from the financial system. Instead, futures allow **risk to move from participants who want less of it to participants willing to accept more of it**. Understanding that relationship prepares us for one of the most important features of futures markets: margin and leverage, which can make futures efficient tools for managing exposure while also creating the possibility of rapid and substantial losses.

Chapter 4: Margin, Leverage, and Risk

Futures markets allow participants to control exposure to substantial quantities of commodities without paying the full value of those commodities upfront. This structure makes futures useful for businesses managing price exposure and traders seeking efficient market access, but it also introduces significant risk. Relatively small price movements can produce large gains or losses compared with the amount of capital committed to a position. Understanding margin, leverage, and risk is therefore essential before participating in commodity futures markets.

How Futures Margin Works

When someone purchases shares of stock outright, the investor generally pays the full purchase price. Futures contracts operate differently.

Instead of paying the entire value represented by a contract, futures participants generally deposit **margin** with their broker.

Futures margin is not the same as making a down payment on the underlying commodity. It functions more like financial collateral that helps ensure the participant can meet the obligations created by the futures position.

The amount required depends on the contract, market conditions, brokerage requirements, and other factors.

Two margin concepts are particularly important.

Initial margin is the amount generally required to establish a futures position.

Maintenance margin is the minimum amount that must remain available to support that position as its value changes.

Futures positions are typically adjusted according to market prices on an ongoing basis through a process known as **marking to market**.

Suppose a trader establishes a futures position and the market moves against it.

The loss is reflected in the trader's account. If the account falls below the required level, additional funds may be necessary to maintain the position.

This can result in a **margin call**.

The trader may need to deposit additional money or reduce or close the position.

If sufficient funds are not available, the broker may liquidate positions according to its policies and applicable market rules.

This system helps manage financial obligations within futures markets, but it also means that losses can require action quickly.

A trader cannot simply assume that an unfavorable position can always be held indefinitely while waiting for the market to recover.

Understanding Leverage and Magnified Gains and Losses

The relationship between the margin deposited and the larger value represented by the futures contract creates **leverage**.

Consider a simplified example.

Suppose a futures contract represents $50,000 worth of a commodity, but the trader is required to maintain only a fraction of that amount to establish the position.

The trader still has price exposure connected to the entire contract value.

If the commodity moves 2 percent, the change in the value of the position could be approximately $1,000 before considering fees and other factors.

Relative to the $50,000 contract value, that movement is modest.

Relative to a much smaller amount of capital supporting the position, however, $1,000 can represent a significant gain or loss.

This is why leverage can be powerful.

It allows participants to obtain substantial market exposure without committing the full notional value of the contract.

For commercial businesses, this can make hedging more capital-efficient.

For speculators, leverage can increase potential returns.

But leverage works equally in the opposite direction.

A relatively small adverse price movement can produce a substantial loss compared with the capital committed to the trade.

Under certain circumstances, losses can exceed the amount initially deposited.

Commodity markets can also move quickly.

Unexpected weather events, geopolitical developments, production disruptions, economic announcements, or changes in government policy can cause significant price movements. Markets can sometimes move sharply between trading sessions or during periods of limited liquidity.

This means leverage should not be viewed simply as a way to increase profit potential.

It is fundamentally a way of increasing **exposure relative to capital**.

That exposure magnifies outcomes regardless of whether those outcomes are favorable.

Managing Risk in Futures Markets

Risk management begins with recognizing that futures trading involves uncertainty.

No analysis can guarantee where commodity prices will move.

A trader can correctly understand supply conditions and still lose money because demand changes unexpectedly. A market can respond differently from what economic logic initially suggests. An unforeseen geopolitical event can completely change expectations.

The first step in **futures risk management** is therefore determining how much loss can reasonably be tolerated.

Position size matters.

Controlling fewer contracts reduces the amount of market exposure compared with controlling many contracts. A trader does not have to use all available leverage simply because the market allows it.

Available capital also matters.

Maintaining only the minimum required margin can leave little room for normal price fluctuations. Keeping additional funds available may provide a larger buffer, although it does not eliminate the possibility of loss.

Participants should also understand the specific commodity they are trading.

Agricultural markets can react sharply to weather forecasts and crop reports.

Energy markets can respond to geopolitical developments, production decisions, inventories, transportation constraints, and seasonal demand.

Metals can be influenced by industrial activity, currencies, interest rates, investment demand, and mining conditions.

Contract expiration creates another source of risk.

A participant who does not intend to become involved in physical settlement must understand when positions need to be closed or rolled. Waiting too long can create complications that were never part of the original strategy.

Traders may also use predetermined exit rules or other techniques intended to limit losses.

However, no risk-management technique provides complete protection.

Markets can move rapidly, and orders intended to exit at a particular price may sometimes be executed at a different price during volatile conditions.

Diversification can reduce dependence on a single position, but commodity markets can become correlated during major economic events.

The most important principle is straightforward: **risk should be considered before a futures position is established, not after the market moves against it**.

A participant should understand the contract, the amount of exposure being taken, the capital available, and the potential consequences of an unfavorable price movement.

For hedgers, risk management also requires looking beyond the futures position itself.

A futures loss may be offset by an improvement in the value of the underlying physical exposure. Evaluating the hedge and physical position together provides a more meaningful picture than looking at either one alone.

Last Thoughts

Margin and leverage are central to the way commodity futures markets operate. Margin allows participants to maintain futures positions without paying the entire value represented by a contract, while leverage creates substantial exposure relative to the capital committed. This structure can make futures efficient tools for hedging and market participation, but it can also magnify losses and create demands for additional capital when markets move unexpectedly. Understanding **position size, available capital, contract specifications, and potential losses** is therefore just as important as understanding where commodity prices might move. With these mechanics established, the next chapter will examine the major commodity groups themselves and why energy, metals, and agricultural futures respond to different economic and physical forces.

Chapter 5: Energy, Metals, and Agricultural Futures

Commodity futures are often discussed as a single market, but the physical commodities behind these contracts can behave very differently. Crude oil responds to refinery demand, production decisions, inventories, and geopolitics. Gold can react to investment demand and interest rates, while copper is closely connected to industrial activity. Agricultural commodities face their own influences, including planting decisions, weather, harvests, and seasonal supply patterns. Understanding these differences is essential because each commodity group has its own economic characteristics and price drivers.

Energy Markets and Their Price Drivers

Energy futures represent some of the most closely followed commodity markets in the world.

Crude oil is particularly important because petroleum remains deeply connected to transportation, manufacturing, chemicals, agriculture, and many other parts of the global economy.

The price of crude oil is influenced by the balance between production and consumption.

On the supply side, production levels can change because of drilling activity, investment decisions, geopolitical events, government policies, maintenance, sanctions, conflicts, and decisions by major producing countries.

Demand can change with economic conditions.

Strong economic activity can increase transportation, manufacturing, and industrial energy consumption. Economic slowdowns can have the opposite effect.

Inventories provide another important signal.

When oil production exceeds immediate consumption, additional barrels may move into storage. When consumption exceeds available production, inventories can decline.

But oil cannot simply be stored anywhere.

Storage tanks, terminals, pipelines, ships, and transportation networks create physical limitations. When storage capacity becomes scarce, unusual pricing conditions can develop.

Natural gas has different characteristics.

Although it is also an energy commodity, **natural gas markets** can be particularly sensitive to weather. Cold winters can increase heating demand, while hot summers can increase electricity demand as air-conditioning use rises.

Storage levels matter because natural gas accumulated during periods of lower demand can help supply periods when consumption increases.

Transportation infrastructure is also important.

Natural gas moves through pipelines and, increasingly, through facilities capable of converting it into liquefied natural gas for transportation by ship. Constraints or disruptions within these systems can affect regional supply and prices.

Refined products such as gasoline and heating fuels introduce another layer.

Crude oil must be processed before becoming many of the fuels consumers actually use. Refinery capacity, maintenance, outages, transportation, and seasonal fuel requirements can therefore influence prices independently of crude oil itself.

Energy markets demonstrate why commodity analysis requires an understanding of the physical system behind the futures contract.

Precious and Industrial Metals

Metals futures cover commodities serving very different purposes.

Precious metals such as gold and silver can be influenced by both physical demand and financial-market conditions.

Gold is used in jewelry, technology, investment products, and official reserves. Unlike commodities that are largely consumed after production, substantial quantities of previously mined gold continue to exist above ground.

This makes investment behavior particularly important.

Interest rates, inflation expectations, currency movements, financial uncertainty, and investor demand can influence gold prices alongside mining production and physical consumption.

Silver has some similar characteristics but also has substantial industrial uses.

As a result, silver can respond both to investment conditions and changes in manufacturing or technological demand.

Industrial metals operate somewhat differently.

Copper, for example, is widely used in construction, electrical systems, manufacturing, transportation, and energy infrastructure.

Because of these applications, **industrial metal demand** can provide information about broader economic activity.

When construction and manufacturing expand, demand for metals may increase. When industrial activity weakens, demand can decline.

Supply can be slow to respond.

Developing a new mine can require years of exploration, permitting, financing, construction, and infrastructure development. Existing mines can also experience disruptions from weather, labor disputes, declining ore quality, equipment problems, or political developments.

Inventories help connect these supply and demand conditions with futures markets.

Low available inventories can make metal prices more sensitive to disruptions. Higher inventories can provide a buffer when supply temporarily exceeds consumption.

Currencies can also matter because many internationally traded commodities are priced in U.S. dollars. Changes in exchange rates can alter purchasing conditions for buyers and producers operating in other currencies.

These factors make metals markets a combination of physical economics and financial-market expectations.

Agricultural Commodities and Seasonality

Agricultural futures introduce another set of market forces because production is closely tied to biological and seasonal cycles.

Corn, wheat, soybeans, and other crops cannot be produced instantly in response to higher prices.

Farmers must decide what to plant, crops require time to grow, and final production depends heavily on conditions throughout the growing season.

This creates **agricultural seasonality**.

Markets can behave differently during planting, growing, and harvesting periods because different information becomes important at each stage.

Before planting, traders may focus on expected acreage and input costs.

During the growing season, weather can become one of the most important influences.

Too little rain can reduce yields. Excessive rainfall can delay planting or damage crops. Extreme heat can create stress during sensitive stages of development.

As harvest approaches, attention shifts increasingly toward actual production and crop quality.

Once crops have been harvested, storage and inventories become important.

Stored grain can help supply consumption until the next harvest, meaning inventory levels can influence how vulnerable the market is to future production problems.

Agricultural demand also comes from several sources.

Crops may be used for human food, livestock feed, industrial processing, exports, and energy-related applications. Changes in any of these areas can influence prices.

Livestock futures add another biological cycle.

Cattle and other livestock require time to breed and raise. Feed costs can influence production decisions, while consumer demand affects the value of the final products.

Diseases, weather, transportation problems, and changes in herd sizes can also affect supply.

These characteristics make agricultural commodities particularly sensitive to timing.

A weather event that would have little effect during one stage of crop development could have major consequences during another.

Seasonality does not mean prices follow the same pattern every year. Rather, it means the underlying production cycle changes which risks and information are most important at different times.

Last Thoughts

Energy, metals, and agricultural futures operate within the same broader futures system, but the physical markets behind them can be remarkably different. Energy prices can respond to production, inventories, infrastructure, and geopolitics. Precious metals combine physical demand with financial influences, while industrial metals are closely connected to manufacturing and economic activity. Agricultural markets introduce weather, biological production cycles, and seasonality. Understanding these differences helps explain why there is no single formula for analyzing commodity futures. The final chapter will bring these markets together by examining **the broader forces that can move commodity prices**, including weather, geopolitical disruptions, inflation, interest rates, currencies, and changes in the global economy.

Chapter 6: What Moves Commodity Futures Markets

Commodity futures prices can move for reasons that extend far beyond the individual commodity itself. Weather can change agricultural production, geopolitical events can disrupt energy supplies, and economic conditions can alter demand across several commodity groups at once. Interest rates, inflation, and currency movements can also influence how commodities are produced, purchased, stored, and valued. Understanding these broader forces helps place individual futures markets within the larger global economy.

Weather, Geopolitics, and Supply Disruptions

Weather is one of the most important sources of uncertainty in many physical commodity markets.

Agriculture provides the clearest example.

Farmers can decide how much land to plant and which crops to grow, but they cannot completely control rainfall, temperature, drought, flooding, storms, or other environmental conditions.

A severe drought in an important growing region can reduce expected production and cause agricultural futures prices to rise. Favorable weather can improve expected yields and place downward pressure on prices.

Weather can also affect energy markets.

Cold winters can increase heating demand, while extremely hot summers can increase electricity consumption. Hurricanes and severe storms can disrupt offshore energy production, refineries, pipelines, ports, and transportation networks.

These events demonstrate the importance of **supply disruptions**.

Commodity markets depend on more than simply producing enough material. Commodities must also be processed, stored, transported, and delivered to the places where they are needed.

A transportation problem can therefore affect prices even when the commodity itself remains available.

A pipeline outage can restrict energy flows. A port disruption can interfere with exports. Railroad or shipping problems can prevent agricultural products from reaching buyers.

Geopolitical events introduce another layer of uncertainty.

Oil, natural gas, metals, and agricultural commodities are traded internationally. Political instability, wars, sanctions, trade restrictions, tariffs, and diplomatic disputes can alter these flows.

The market often reacts before the full consequences are known.

If traders believe a geopolitical event could reduce future oil exports, for example, futures prices may rise even while physical supplies continue moving normally.

This reflects the forward-looking nature of futures markets.

Participants are not only responding to what has already happened. They are continuously evaluating what could happen next.

That can create volatility when uncertainty is particularly high.

Inflation, Interest Rates, and Currency Movements

Commodities are closely connected to inflation because energy, food, metals, and other raw materials contribute to costs throughout the economy.

Rising commodity prices can increase transportation, manufacturing, construction, agricultural, and consumer costs.

At the same time, **inflation** can influence commodity markets.

When investors become concerned about declining purchasing power, some may increase their exposure to certain commodities, particularly precious metals.

The relationship is not always straightforward.

Commodity prices can rise during inflationary periods, but different commodities may respond differently depending on supply, demand, economic growth, inventories, and financial conditions.

Interest rates add another influence.

Higher **interest rates** increase the cost of borrowing money. This can affect businesses, consumers, commodity producers, and investors.

Rates can also influence the cost of carrying physical inventories.

If a business borrows money to purchase and store a commodity, higher financing costs can make holding that inventory more expensive.

Interest rates may also affect investment demand.

Assets that generate interest can become more attractive when rates rise, potentially changing investor interest in commodities that do not produce income.

Currency movements are equally important.

Many internationally traded commodities are priced in U.S. dollars. As a result, changes in the **U.S. dollar** can influence purchasing conditions around the world.

If the dollar strengthens against another currency, a dollar-priced commodity can become more expensive for buyers using that other currency, even if the commodity's dollar price does not change.

A weaker dollar can create the opposite effect.

Currency movements can also affect producers.

A mining company might sell its output in dollars while paying wages and other expenses in a local currency. Changes in exchange rates can therefore influence profitability and production decisions.

This connection between commodities, interest rates, inflation, and currencies demonstrates why futures markets cannot be analyzed entirely in isolation.

They exist within a much larger financial system.

Reading Commodity Markets in the Larger Economy

Commodity markets can provide useful information about conditions in the broader economy.

Industrial commodities are particularly relevant.

Copper, energy, and other materials are used throughout construction, manufacturing, transportation, and infrastructure. Changes in demand can sometimes reflect changes in economic activity.

Strong industrial growth may increase consumption of raw materials.

A slowdown can reduce demand.

Agricultural and energy prices can also influence household spending because food, transportation, heating, and electricity are important expenses.

This creates a two-way relationship.

Economic conditions influence commodity prices, and commodity prices can influence economic conditions.

A sharp increase in energy prices, for example, can raise costs for businesses and households. Transportation becomes more expensive. Manufacturers may face higher production costs.

Consumers may have less money available for other purchases.

Commodity markets can therefore become part of the transmission of economic shocks.

However, interpreting commodity prices requires caution.

A rising oil price does not automatically mean the global economy is strengthening. Prices could instead be rising because production has been disrupted.

A falling copper price does not automatically signal recession. New supply or changes within the industry could also influence the market.

This is why **economic context** matters.

Rather than interpreting a commodity price movement by itself, it can be useful to consider what is happening with production, inventories, demand, currencies, interest rates, transportation, and the wider economy.

Relationships between different commodities can provide additional information.

Rising energy and agricultural prices may indicate very different conditions from rising industrial metals prices. Precious metals may respond to financial uncertainty even while economically sensitive commodities weaken.

Futures curves can add another layer by showing how markets value different delivery periods.

Together, these signals can provide insight into how market participants currently perceive supply, demand, risk, and economic conditions.

They are not perfect forecasting tools.

Markets can be wrong, expectations can change, and unexpected events can quickly alter the outlook.

The value of commodity futures is not that they provide a guaranteed view of the future. It is that they continuously bring together information and expectations from participants throughout the physical and financial economy.

Last Thoughts

Commodity futures markets are influenced by an interconnected set of forces. Weather can change production, geopolitical events can disrupt trade, inflation and interest rates can alter financial conditions, and currencies can change the economics of buying and selling commodities internationally. At the same time, movements in energy, metals, and agricultural markets can provide information about what is happening throughout the broader economy. Understanding these relationships makes it easier to see commodity futures as more than trading instruments. They are part of a global system through which **physical supply, economic**

demand, financial conditions, and expectations about the future continually interact to create prices.

Last Thoughts: Understanding Futures Before Participating

Commodity futures markets play an important role in the global economy. They help producers, businesses, and other commercial participants manage uncertainty while giving traders and investors a marketplace for expressing expectations about future commodity prices. Throughout this book, we have seen that futures are much more than instruments for speculation. They are part of the system through which commodities are priced, risks are transferred, and information about physical markets is reflected in financial markets.

A futures contract may appear relatively simple at first.

A buyer takes one side.

A seller takes the other.

The price moves as market conditions change.

But behind that contract is a much larger economic system.

Crude oil futures are connected to production, refineries, transportation networks, inventories, and global energy demand.

Copper futures are connected to mines, manufacturers, construction, electrical infrastructure, and industrial activity.

Agricultural futures are connected to farmers, weather, harvests, storage facilities, food producers, livestock operations, and consumers.

Understanding these physical connections is one of the most important parts of understanding commodity futures.

The market price on a screen represents the interaction of thousands of decisions being made throughout this system.

Producers are deciding how much to produce.

Businesses are estimating future costs.

Commercial users are managing inventories.

Traders are interpreting new information.

Investors are responding to economic conditions.

All of these participants can influence the process through which futures prices are established.

This is why understanding the market itself should come before attempting to predict where prices will go.

A trader might correctly identify a commodity with strong long-term demand and still experience losses because the futures contract was purchased at an unfavorable price.

A producer might believe prices will increase but still choose to hedge because protecting an acceptable selling price is more important than maximizing potential revenue.

A manufacturer might willingly accept a loss on a futures position because falling commodity prices simultaneously reduced the cost of its physical purchases.

Context changes how futures positions should be evaluated.

The same principle applies to contango and backwardation.

Neither condition automatically tells someone whether to buy or sell. Instead, these structures provide information about how the market is pricing commodities across different periods.

The same is true of inventories, weather reports, economic data, currencies, and geopolitical developments.

They provide information.

They do not provide certainty.

That distinction becomes particularly important because futures involve leverage.

A person can control commodity exposure worth considerably more than the capital initially required to maintain the position. This makes futures efficient, but it also means that mistakes can become expensive quickly.

Small movements in the underlying commodity can translate into substantial changes in the value of a futures position.

For that reason, understanding **risk before return** is essential.

Before participating, a market participant should understand what the contract represents, how large the exposure is, when the contract expires, how settlement works, what margin requirements apply, and what could happen if the market moves sharply in the opposite direction.

Understanding the underlying commodity matters just as much.

Oil should not be analyzed exactly like gold.

Gold should not be analyzed exactly like copper.

Copper should not be analyzed exactly like wheat.

Every commodity has its own production system, demand structure, inventory characteristics, transportation requirements, seasonal influences, and market participants.

That is part of what makes commodity futures markets both complex and valuable.

They provide a window into the physical economy.

Movements in commodity markets can reflect changing expectations about manufacturing, agriculture, energy demand, inflation, global trade, weather, economic growth, and geopolitical risk.

But futures markets should not be treated as perfect forecasting systems.

Prices represent the collective expectations of market participants based on currently available information. Those expectations can change rapidly when new information arrives.

Understanding this uncertainty is part of understanding the market.

For businesses, futures can provide tools for managing it.

For speculators, futures provide opportunities to accept it.

For investors and economic observers, futures markets can provide information about how participants are interpreting it.

The most important lesson is therefore not how to predict the next movement in crude oil, gold, copper, corn, or any other commodity.

It is understanding the structure behind those movements.

Commodity futures connect **supply and demand, physical production, financial markets, risk management, and expectations about the future**. Once those relationships are understood, the prices appearing on a futures screen become more meaningful.

That understanding should come before participation.

Futures can be valuable tools, but they are leveraged financial instruments with meaningful risks. Knowledge does not eliminate those risks. It provides a stronger foundation for recognizing them, evaluating them, and making more informed decisions about whether and how commodity futures belong within a broader financial or business strategy.

About the Author

Roggie "Raj" Clark is an entrepreneur and a 10-year marketing professional with a proven track record in e-commerce and digital business growth. Having built and managed successful online stores with thousands of sales and consulted for numerous marketing clients, Roggie has mastered the intricacies of online marketing, branding, and consumer behavior. He has also written several popular books on digital marketing, SEO (search engine optimization), and programming (HTML, CSS, and JavaScript).

As a former marketing manager at a fintech company—a role he secured through his own marketing and financial expertise—Roggie gained firsthand experience in financial strategy and wealth-building. This journey inspired him to share insights with amateur investors, helping them save money, make smarter financial decisions, and build long-term wealth. Raj currently lives in Maryland with his sister and niece.

www.ingramcontent.com/pod-product-compliance
Lightning Source LLC
LaVergne TN
LVHW050747061126
851857LV00013B/1031